PROPELLER BOOKS CONTEMPORARY POETRY SERIES
EDITORS *Lucas Bernhardt and Jan Verberkmoes*

DEAR WEIRDO

Abraham Smith

PROPELLER BOOKS

PORTLAND, OREGON • UNITED STATES OF AMERICA

First U.S. Edition, 2022

Copyright © 2022 by Abraham Smith

All rights reserved. No part of this book may be used or reproduced in any manner whatsoever without written permission from the publisher, except in the case of brief quotations embodied in critical articles or reviews.

For further information, contact Propeller Books,
4325 Northeast Davis Street, Portland, OR 97213.

Cover and interior design by Context

Published by Propeller Books, Portland, Oregon.
ISBN 978-0-98277-048-1

www.propellerbooks.com

In Memoriam: Brad Watson & Monica Detra & Craig Arnold

For Nathan Parker

For Charlie Parr

For my Snarlin' Yarn Fam: Fiddlerbee/Lil Bird\Jaybird/Colonel\ Tomatillo/Janager

DEAR WEIRDO

PICK A STICK UP THESE DAYS AND IT'S SNAKES
and here it turns out we'll be just shy
of eternally gone
almost always have been
sewin masks from notso longgo gone
grumpy gramsy's quilt stash now
hear this said dasn't for
you had better not
said warsh for wash
had an ear issue had one eye
when young they booted her
back of the class couldn't hear
teacher her mastoid mastered her
she was left out put upon she was
the oldest she shouldered it
enjoyed a giant halfoff sweetroll
like her children after her
fake wrote while squint listened
her whole life after at the back
ran the 40 yard dash in 0
the 1 time rutabaga got away
in town his leash ribboning behind
him like diesel out the tailpipe in cold
and we sang in church like a wheel
rubbin on somethin and the glass

stained sparrowier somethin like celery
gone bad in a ditch fulla 13dayold
pictures of chased and chased whales
with one so-so tire i re-member chaos-ity
of windowraisin flies she won
the negativity doorsize trophy again
had a coupon for cold cold rain
if a breeze then a bad one if a sun then a bad sun
what can i say?? she saved my robinweep skin
from my own 2 hands a million
she was cripes but she was the same cripes
each and each and ever day
she was the only place
my blood could hang gentle in my skin
fern comb the trillium and this
here pisstrail dance it in
on over into nothin
but sugar cookies
and how we almost
butchered the tupperware
to get on in cock chin and
like the larger birds sing
crazy as 16 '61 dryers
fulla frozen blubber
chawin in the attic
here in harm nation
it's hard not to thin thinkin
of the body ma as a broken coffeepot
one those old aluminum sneaky light percolator jobs

them rattail hard kids use to scoop rock creek crayfish
trick is they hit gas in reverse and there ain't
anythin much more human than
our great wide shadow circling down
shading cup on up over the sun
bull shake hand what we done can't be undone
people season perpetual storm
phone spine bent platte river sunflower
stuccoed malicious in snow ices
soon the nose will cut the heart open
and blood will too run circular
hot gold down the throat
reach for the egg under the hen
and schist that's a snake too
of the bull snake variety can't be blamed
warm is warm is warm is warm
even when yr roof's a dawngonegonzo fidget spinner hey
hey it's jughead life ma and i hate to see
you smellin like some rubber stood up on
while leg trap snap hearts freak behind
sling wink bar javelin got a boomerang tendency
and in some countries it ain't even new moon noon
briefest taste watchful jail lights surge weave
we've ez-mail-in made a sugar self
at rat rant expense of all others
dished and steamin you still workin??
tell me when to take it away
it is the eyepatch over yr fear heart
it tar the monsanto tailings oaten in my low brow rite shoe

just try and dream on that santa sky med just try
when all's you see in sleep is seep by some shedding sandstone
and a wolf with a housecat she's
cleanin down to tasty there there
cat come to water
more ways than lug lungs alone
stoopt among potato hills
before nobody so much as crow
in red pine givin the body word
we all come to be by
so many caw came to be
beside the river wye caw
beatup hootmouth waterboy caw
pointin the way caw
with the catpee maw of
his broken open right shoe caw
cellar oil spoil a sandstorm
ooh blood uu feathered heel
there's red in you so green
seems to do the yoga
with dinosaurs
staked leash tacked in
slurry roadcut gravel i'll be
this shapely traveler wanders on
thru slew and bough and gnome moss numb
now who got their mood foot
on my loose thread?? do
the mummy hoodoo?? not
with radical gratitudes ma

spurtin the maggots too
off saddle glad path
it's said time is the monarch
one wing half ate by robin
turnin and turnin
like the fancy hotel door
where execs blow farts
before stridin in chin out
like the barkbeetle in bark
said time is the bear walks
like there's a family in each leg
like a vowel leakin all over a word
it's said time is the PTO shaft
no matter how slow bound to reel u in
it's said it'll fetch yr overhauls clear off
and shall you bee saved by washrot cloth??
a kid in a war dream shovels good
guy teeth from lost arm shore
it's said you'll be found in yr birthday suit
muddle of the field not a mark on ya
with the sky shuckin hawks and the other offhand birds
somehow born to be exploded judge robe
and bootlegger boot lace on high
said yer getting there
when ya rub onion skins
on yr teeth what could be sexier
than the hopechest on fire?? and was that
my sandwich or yr hand?? go
book a read backwards

go try flip skinny pages
til true wrinkles unski off the skin
and innocences retread
newest dust in america
upheld by tremblin peachfuss
robin pronouncin newday
with an umlaut over the dream of
the invention of a first plow
fashioned from hawk's-wing
dragged along prairie scathed no
unzipt no held shut rooted in as is
only higher artemisia nova a little tickled
tickz the bees off it's 8 9 seconds
when things resettle
it's a picnic of slippery fish
spelled in place with a kicked can
fulla backwater my earliest memory
i am before grades at the mount there's a patch of grasses
lush as only a season of forgotten rain could bring
storm lode a mother ring ring
the watcher hey you kids go collide there
and i go to take a drink of pepsi free
when a bumble bee kittens
from the sip hole all bear den sleepy
in a trashsack for clothes
rides her thorn on to who knows
and i begin again to arbor uncut the imago
costs you reader pal based off all this
wash of flat rate chat to come

maybe less than the lyric faucet leak whose
rounding pearl gets a gutful and
descends quieter than a sunflower
seed down a ballplayer deep
deep leftfield ol gimpshrimp at the plate
old ueck on one them sidewinder tales
where he's tryin to tell it all by tellin
what it wasn't and he's stuck on that's
just the way it was guys then guys then and here it's
3 and 1 when you thought it was
maybe 0 and 1 and the other guy
no relation to wisconsin
has a voice wants nothin more
than to get on back home
to the chitown burbs where
maybe his wife is waitin up
and maybe she never rehit
the dryer button so when he
reaches in for his pj's they feel
like bein forsaken if that isn't
too much to say out
which then awakens siri
and then his wife is up
and once she's dawn at dark
the only technique is xanax
with a bailey's chaser and
the slower purr of the dryer
and the click of the buttons
on the pj's it's all right now

life is a beautiful thing click like
fingernails on glass
nails on a glass table
cigarette in the other hand
if you will listen is talkin
the language of plastic squeezin
around and around a dead toe and
what cards might i have drawn different
had i took that job in kokomo?? and
how goes yr mathmind wind?? and
is tomorrow actually another day cat?? or
is countin sexy?? ueck don't seem
to think so but this
this we do know
rob deer is out and trottin
back to the outfield like he did
33 too many squats in his sleep
and the ghostest with the mostest
old dandelion mic
precarious as an old fart on ice prays
kicksing welder bellstar ticktickin swimmin hole
toaded turded teaked teach me
the folded napkin the sheeting tuck
the everything so hospital perfect
until no ma it's not
last year remodel like new
barley harley tell me honey ethanol epipen
where's that bumble gone??
long about half the buzz there was

gone gone
the blues these days go the wide world round
the painters over the fences
and the brushes tunet to pokin sticks for nothin
finer than kid spites on pets hateful of fences
and that cat doublenamed for spring dreams every fence afire
how then let the flowers talk to flowers??
well way i heard it from youtube is
hold yr breath faceplant in paint bowl
and go out walkin soppin and drippin
to sousaphone them little blarers
with none but yr mousenest hair brites the cage
buncha lichened elk ribs from which to build
a boat afore ya drown in slow sand and
god is a buffalo chewin on a phonebook beside margo price
keeps on snowing sky high cry eye
in them bad old days between the stems
of two three bitter oleanders knives
and forks and spoons climbin thrown
up fishin line the wind takes to fumblin
there upon the first front porch
i can think of trick out no better future
for my bones than windchimes
translatin obeisance into somethin
danceable go on up and ride yr ghost mule y'all
all over porchy graveyard
computer chairs gettin their lean on
and tho the chairs may preserve the languaged
angle of the accident and tho the old

dogs stunt fat tight as woodticks
fit to burst from lumberjack anger blood
no you can't
cut 'em mad can't get at a
mintbritch towerer cheekbit like that
else ol pine'll sense it and ol woodpecker too
fallin as she flies with the moody maestro move
of the chinese factory machine sews
faux sequin pockets into denim cough asses
but ain't a sequin faux glory to begin with??
pralines this dagger crocus teacher chipmunk
inhaled too much ether for a barrelfire tuesday
and this here white pine tastes a little like marten blood
dottin dimples over halffroze springfed creek rabbit coyote
if i am preachin honest chainsaw buck bucks like tryin to
endless hold a totally pissed big pike fish and what seemed
so slow to start to tip gets sudden up upon ya
as in dentist xray aprons flyin
from the closet much haste moth sunder
square upon the screwed drool of yr heart
and just like everything everything flares as it outgoes itself
ol patchy dog too meaned thru from all that livin room livin
sandbag ricefling riots self gainst the big baywindow
while pokemon go funsters with them stapleguns
frozen in sidewalk ice for eyes in sponge bob pajama bottoms
whose stains recall aerial views of ioway pig farms
scoop and stoop and snoop and starve grace out
wren breads no wren bowls no wren alights
like a painful to henry david thoreau

palmful of pencil dust yes aspback snow
phantom limning birch's bronchials
walks a hankie out a train window in a movie
there's a cut in wrist could bleed snow
mm such rotsweet partings starrin
fate's wirin in need of some crossin
gets to sparkin the smoke in ringlets
this arthritic bobcat out by the blown
hottub works perfectly fine if you had a motor
you could hook it to the birch and get it
growled up faster world needs
more ghosts when
timed skin gets to achin
spall is his gut rewatchin
constipated rocky with the
afghanistan twitches and a picture
on his phone of himself
with a knife has it hard
way it's not able to love anythin
out enterin the thing
has a facthead like a too much erased crossword
banana peel in the right hand it does get harder now
not to see a knife in everything wilted
by time's patient urge brines
goalpost leanin like a giraffe drunk on her own urine
fracksand piled high might even be
warhead back out over there
in his mental eye acts a corner
painter fool catchin at the grit blown

see that's what they call a perfectly round sand
and the farmer pasture gouged like a bear
through ant rot log to the maniac hive
i ain't gonna lie to you you stock those hole
with manatee with telescopes for snorkel airsip
in a mt dew taurine xodream sand trucks
go bears from dogs them sand trains piled high
preachin christmas tell it mama choochoo
who got rich who got rich who
i know i hear them clipped grasses
layin down side beside the perpetual motion
of a perfect roundness loped to a laughtrack
say now was that just jim putzin by in a new ford?? why yes
he sold his pasture to the gouge man for a round sand
and u cud dew much worse
born luck enuff to retire on rounds to coax
old t rex gelatin outta a stale hole and
he still counts cuts the gridiron grasses
tho ain't nobody played there in years
unless you could number rick and terri thinner
than sandhill crane sculptures
made of clotheshangers and solder wire
them burnhole flannels jumpin off 'em
some kinda freak freedom squirrel
burnbarrel fire in a quick wind
crackin each other up about a gif meme
while the vape smoke billows grapely
like the sky over gary indiany and
their kid named after a lichen

the kind'll eat yr socks and
crack jokes about the moonlight on the pliers
jacked on grape soda
tumbles after moth or butterfly
afloat like the angel pringle
detonates dandelion afterlives
don't make me say it again
gotta get back to home so we can sit down
no he never was one for showy
on his touchdowndance just set the ball down
like he was duty laying landmines out because it's the right
thing to do meth movin through like wolves did once
light widens this much credit plasstic breaks
waxy bandits swimmin in from higher
somewhere vices pluto cold turn and turn
blue jaws in and in
they don't much eat 'em as hold
a world size-ier than their hearts silly
careful between parted beaks and
in one pez head felt tilt way
man that one really dug in
talkin about the berry down the hatch
of the waxwing and i know you've
heard all this before but the berries
are off their heads and the birdies
early on cardshuffle foxhotwaterbottle
slowly go the clay of the drunk
gambler's shufflin hands right now
you could reach out and take one drunk one

cheapo pepper grinder or the hollow spine
of the unspooled papertowel roll
you was savin for a culvert when
it's time to buy no build the farm how
knot be wooden when you've finished
fratgoldfishing those jawgigglers down?? and
who ever was plangent mornings after a bfast
of burnt toast and frozen coffee?? come
a rest stop of shoetrees upon the mind
come dh lawrence steppin out back into
the horsehay light with one suspender down
and a on fire cough chest thin as
that ny statute of liberation weldwand
seen reflected thru
shark cake fin bay wave brief arisen
by a broker's powerboat so no
actual natural wave after all endless tho
as frank lloyd wright goin on about
frank lloyd wright
then the air give a chronic sound
as if the oldest bulldog bullfrog won a chickenknuckle
cravat or hinge
let that spoon of eyecrust and castor oil
pond fob decide breath be my eyes
neck made to sky
five cranes calligraph the great wide
bunch and bind then one wing ticks another
offkilter quarter bookshelf times timed vines vase and mantel
waddled by the aftershocks' reptilian trundlebed

sleeps three in the dream of lecithin sardine
look here it's 99 if 9 dead
asian ladybug beetles
all capsule pill squeezable
in this ghost hat ceramic
wasn't finest happy birthday gesture aver
subtle gotyou latenight kidtag
i find i watch how fruits grow
for what time is it?? quarter to
the legs off banquet tables burning
must run under thru my legs
if i am to be statue no more
why they somersault inside
sugar furious around the round
let my blood's field to the labyrinth people
whose sure walk is meant to mirror the human gut
ineluctable to the drop zone
while the mind above never mind it
wants the vascular addle of a snakegag ball
not even the dog is known to go for no more
heart remarkably gutbound by lack of adventure
it is written right there in the book of what
to expect the width of the berry
betides the night's narcoleptic rooster
where lost we walked wolfish dog
and whistled for comfort no one returning we are free
life goes ready wing it
best prize is in wing it
expression of a gull

after a bad chicken wing
horseshoes is over
get over it cornhole is king now at night we
underarm dinner scraps into
window's mossbacks unta
the passenger cranberry spider fattening at the center
the second after tha match gits struck
gentles a roof on this captured morning brings
what light and wind will all
over surfaces holes all
over holes surfaces
the trick is no trick try this
there's a cave halfwayup and
around the side burned by wind
dripping in time
to the squirrel tacking up the locust
and the blood is a river stranger than gasoline
and knowing doesn't always beam a word
close around one
just to see what you feel
i close around the word just to feel what you feel
and it occurs to us
there is no aging there are
only bad decisions
o this new snow falling
no a crow falls can tell it
by one will lift one way down
the down's neat pile
the clip-on tie the correct

candor for mourning
one can
attach to dear old gone friends
the peas' leonine torches touchin night loosely
by trying the gait on i try not to hate
steppa patty by splaying my feet
like he did this is a duck walk
some thin ice this elf rat is pure
this here is an opening down where
velvet grows and woodchucks scuff
this was once for nutmeats now looks like
how to accuse or nudge the needle on
say it aging is singin to the skips more
cry out in crumb of sandy empty
skips let the music be
poor invite to iris if only
night were just an above ground
swimmin pool seeded with rotten bananas and
aging is enjoyin baths more true
and more there is no one
to reach nothing to email
womb and tomb
as i submerge
through the silencing
whiffling steam
into the love you hawt water
am i not practicing
for the fire
they will slide me into

the very one eddy says he refuses
you know i want
to take up some
space after he says serious
between brown sips nodding
at himself in
the darkened kitchen window
on a thursday
unlike any other
the windows no longer
smeared by oils
from hands
once the highest
his kids could reach
rise hair rise shoulder rise body
rise table rise chair rise mattress rise mare
rise mayor upon a stove of butterfly bandaids
this spray of dragonflies 2 unbolt the doghair
from your power is no suchathing
in a barren barrel sharin needles
with shot fishes let justice
for the windpipe let justice for the mama spine
let justice for the bladder relaxing ahead of its time
let justice for the father heart rent falling open
windfall apple in the blind gut wild hog
whose gore tusks need saw now
or gig own grave open season on souueee
pound the wind like a dough dude
do let the chips' reruns go do

the splits upon empty boxin ring floor
eyed like a rite wide peacock tail
with them electrocution dimes
and it gets harder still
later early to laud calm ma
tho to ear the
oldtimers and welloffenoughs tell it
jist waitye for time to lick the apple bad clean
when our time ain't any kind fallin rain
sez the manhole to the digital peekhole
shark gun fin gut herd expiate
long the lord road to no tellin
while clouds no smokes
fur the farther nearer quick as
jump twitch body bodies
seconds before dreams
of all these icetrays to fill
all these trays and your
only little helper the one
stunned bullhead's molten left eye
and the light dim seen
as a forked religiously egg
marauded upon by jakeleg ants
seems they got the sugar shits 24/heaven
you got dat rite proffers ezchaired paul
himself turned to blocky ash shook
into the river he often did his eyes up at
like that was tha skunk schoonerin tru da garden
for hooks in trees and broken lines and lost lunkers

pullin the very wet out his heart
held up to misfortune's light
crystal spine bonvivants myrrth color
spankt by juicebox joy
swelled against the bick wall
of bullshit opinions go on and
recite the mystery story again
of chantrelles livin the skintag american dream
all over sandbar chair that's that take er as she goes river
don't so much mind the carry by try anythin twice
body boot bark barn yarn carp cameo cart
from the shop&gob down by the petered boothphone
aw ma do you remember
when you had to happen
upon what you had to say?? leg it loiter
enter as in a mri tube
yr gas can rag heart all up in yr ears
the nervous hearse speechtalk curlin up the neckbones
while outside this upright glass coffin
none other than insect tall pieces of rain ah
the future is all about chewin bubblegum bubblewrappin
with yr eyes and far as i can tell they oughta call
every singlet one popopop romance river
waxen heart shout chest
fitful muskrat burnished witchhat
must be those weasel dream again
romance on the river road honestly
i just peed and worse behind the bar hat sign
i see just people are museums of their hungers

i just seen the guy with the grenade tattoo over
his adam's apple poopin his hotrod wheel
round for round i want a car shape of a tear
down the neckhole of a gto bear
and yes i am still intent on a resay
one those midlife drunk ascetics
jumpin a yardstick
with a heart problem
me or stick i ain't sayin
pug some mystery in inn
if at all possible make your sunflower
of rebar and of tractor reactor disc bullshit
and of autumn why let me tell it
i to you a dew a spoon
claimin central standard up on a mountain pass
autumn comes
to everybody's pocketos why i read it
just today in these here covidian hunker blinds
blam blam the rich shootin us down
like in duckhunt the billionaires
upped their kitty ante 33% in just
march to nov 20/20 roar ro-a-oar
how about that??
foodline stretched along the wide earth
like a weakenin hernia stitch
these ultra of this cornfuck land
hear they gettin injections
of babycalftonguefat in their eyelids sorry porch
for sayin it but the circulars do add up

pile mousy piss brown junk up
in later november say
their richy cedar pockets see
gunna get a little ticklish then fell swall away
in my repeater dream anyhay
sneezes jesus with one swift ripping tingle
the streets sudden come alive
i said go out for a pass not for a piss
all hungover eggeye last cube in the tray see
didn't get used so it's swimeye parade mornings
with everybody losing their overdraft balance doin
the natural gas dinosaur dip dip
but who stands up fast on a pill like that??
and i have no idea how come this chair
yet here it is dryin out fruitwise like them soaked up sippers
shaken pained run tha bust barrel bastard basement claim
wide open burns the bleed
gonna slow gotta last first time dawn
beats a beak up along the prayin mattress
proud and tall and green course
there's a certain gorse horseface snorts
a golf ball sound comes
with cold and so-called solid items
settling in construction silt
up along the gills of denial and pride
now did regret just try and do that??
cement britches backwards bicker sing
be the crayfish only softer this
sit up to burp in bed music feels

a little like the wicker parts
of every song you didn't have
to grow to love catch fire
feeble at first old dog
all bone no meat
ya coulda strucka match
on the flint of his last days
gone puppy gas splash sudden manna
no bone all meat laid out
in the scraps dish licked
beyond mirrorness
by what could have been named zeal
flopped and bleeding casual
as a hs senior on some sawdust
for that perfect last snap of babyfat
with a lonesome birch arm propped
like a castoff cast on some haycrud behind
hot water bottle jiggling take these
ellipses of eel bladder for homeplate
parts of song body partings
this one here is ochre hair
this one boast skin this one human
liquid run through a cutlass
by timed name of ardor ardmore okay
cheap ass smokes broken tato chips
funyon asleep forever gotcha licorice sticky
down that little dark night slit
unto the parkin brake's cheaper metals
practice best they can keepin the feel

of the outside air in until you bum bump
into some body and when ya kwik whip around
ol whiplash has a cousin sound and
eyes the size of alabama mississippi
eyes size of in between
ess-curved and oxbowed by nowhere creases
ain't no bizness casual collar pops quite like
kite eyes size of cartoon dogs and
there she is yes there she is for love for life
or for this cigliplife tonight
a lovely somebody
smoking bees from a pipe cup bone
enhanced in shine
by bowling alley sheen ran
fingers thru the plastic intelligences
of the dead chicken chip bag
and thence down lane wood so sop fine
beechtree's taste for growin broken boxin gloves
can get a little obnoxious obvious i know it ma
and here i thought the coda clay limbs
was busy dreamin
clowns paintin rivers
covered up in toilet paper swans
rabbited radishes for broader
gauzy stretcher cloud strokes
be bold about what you do totem
but don't you never forget old brick gotta
stomach fulla loose sand old buick
whose roof fabrics billow down

jelly fish chandeliers
it's 5pm in the middle of the atlantic
u betcha u buncha aspen plinko fingerz
and there's a caraway faraway
everything comes to one and there's a stump
with a sandwich leanin on it and
there's a wild dog happy hesitant
and there's a dog hair texture to maybe
when no is actual meant
mind of its own my oatmeal bowl
there's a trap in every good good thing
this one goes out to
all them glass chin chauvinists
livin in 1980 1890
be damned
love don't got yr sweat under area impressionable tongue
i am wellish grassy tasty cold grey stone
i am good it is struck by light gush
to be walking with you and there's this
to say no body does crooked straighter
than a beech they used to throw old hank in
jail sometimes to dry him out there's that
icon shot of him shirtless and
out of plumb like a kicked fence wry scrawn
you know some folks are these helpless houseplants
on balconies forgot about by the people
and whipped by elements and schooled
by roof no rain reaches a staplefang
fact old hank was seed on fastforward

fruit dictation whim cheat escutcheon
leads with cow parsnip rash o' dewclaw
why we tearsing tireswing away
to a lakeside of breezes keeps the flies off
reach on up up go easy handle all that passin
just as casual as the door to the bathroom
now was there ever really a door or was knob
only a nob of the mind?? stranger street
there she walks hipnotized static broom never met her nose
when you ain't sick nothin goin
it's wednesday at 3:33:33 and you've been
peein regular all day all those
caffeine bursts so behind you
and the woman storker
and the man mountain hamburger
swabbin the decks of short park grass
with little purple plastic bags
like they're wipin the ass off the world
with an old man with a drinker problem's nose
and the dogs look out yes they have something big
to tell there once was a fox name of chagrin
whose pickaxe dh lawrence beard shadow somehow
seem'd to cobcorn sweeteat the thin ankles
of motor oil slickhair wayne thinkin
i need a name change to wade
wait what about walk on rainbow pigeon water??
and these two foxy barkers put up hands a little
in praise in praise get down a little more now
there is a firmer somewhere

to get down in this slush stygian
do the low crawl shit a fifth leg
shit a parking brake is it strange
to be confronted?? comforted by the warmth
reaching up through your hand
from your dog's worked for partings
shat a hand to have and hold
for there is no ecstasy
like the ecstasy of dogs after a fine one
alighter they leap and laugh aloud
and look behind and kick the dust or snow
and break every human rule regardin
future's past now bet on it ma bent on
pitiful guarded decorum
ain't that a shame?? best get back to my ratkillin
ah but would that we could take the lesson
do together what one apart never can
next time dear shy-no why not leap
why not click socked heels honk the harmonica
packt with glitter of fishscales
honk it hard louder passion's not a problem
lard larder free pair you kin
afford to be a lil cavalier go
to the dog heart doctor a little less
lay down those kmart proofreadin glasses
alarmed to find themselves dust's manger
and join me over here there is
no expiration i can find
to this fruit loop stalagmite couch thrift lamp

curious or stricken or born to lean or
bored w/ reasonin w/ even tides
chop chop what is thine soul??
broken hard cinnamon candy on the sidewalk
over which nerves the screwdriver
of the season pirate tourniquet waxwing
thatthat thatthat that is mine
punch those grouse neck grease years in
even eyelid meat
the height of a h
has a timetone monochromatic
but so there
as kids we played church
potato chips for the eucharist grapejuice
from concentrate for the wine
difference was we invented funny walks
from the pew down the aisle to the doler
of the heaventoast i had one i did i squirmed
like a bug halfstoned on some mold under
a roof tile tossed by the bad storm of 84
and that was me rememberin my body
thru george jefferson on that tv show
somethin about jetfuel at the hip
about candor's candy and believe you me
from showout to showdown in the time
a hickory switch blows down you
don't advertise there is no homemade sign
with weird ass apostrophe but you do it you raise perch
bluegill in pisa lean boots

tall as the necks of tammy and george
stackt ones on tops of others and
i've heard it said each number one duet
hit comes with another giraffebone graft it's hard
because they fail they spill
they quail on a pin cushion
cry cry cry thank god brite lake is
but steps away early i might well be
nobody see the fog unsays me out
on riotgreen edges kleenex genie heron
stiller than the spines in the covid morgues
fill and wing fill and wing
rachel carson furred in keyhole
plastic lint shelf doom can't rest wild
intenser minus arm storms and no words
for black and gold and green
accordioning to the precancer light
heron notions heron rips on off across
the bandaid way
heron torrent listenin to menu options
for insurance on the nuclear telephone press 9
arrest 6 mash white 3
flew from within within
and was what you bodysought
that haunted?? longbird flowin the sky
pondersome thicksome sleeknit
my that britannica crowd does burn slow
scissored ram fro-zen toiletpaper
cross-stitched diff between decidin to and doin

all wrapped up in ivory carves of flight
in trophy's slush ice in bone's smoke flank in heavy lie's
chalkline inside whose sad country the hope snow
grows certain daring faces tonight just follow the plan
and all will be ok tends to mean
be careful be grateful for yr supper
of the memory or echo of somebody
making farting noises with their armpits
i am so happy sorry to be lost
in this parking lot with you feels right
did our hands just touch??
clothespin wind lashin side down
two birds with beaks of wood kissin slivers
in a mutual of omaha barn door burn store
phoebe or spent wren?? swept up schooled away
it's to carbeepbeeeep we move for maybe
move as mountains move
under bison hooves
through desert sunset
nudie suit bright
the roger miller line bukka white
neither 1 of us can remember
back of a lawnmower t model ford
mayfly arising like a stroke victim
to hit the head or did ya just pee in the closet??
toward the crescent city canopener moon ma
tell it mighty tell it slow tell it like a confession
into the suncrack steerin wheel while this mars red train
backs up again gonna show ya that caboose yet before ya

make the bank with yr sackcloth sorryhole
and who among us isn't a big soup can with a baby on it
after all?? baby benchpressin
the owlyarnball too
her miracle fierce toes
holding to
the mouse skulls inside
these are my prides
foreplay of dusts most days stir while heatin
some floorlength credence
crudescence you cleamed nee just by walkin
toward me long ago last call
was a rooster roarin armageddon
at the firefly convention
folks fall asleep counting
begin again at one
it's always just startin
this beg riot in the kitchen
this meg ryan ramble with the lantern
held out front of nowhere
walk yr way past judgments
freest as the beeches
dismantled of crows those
thickset samovar of night
the truth of a tree is it grows with great violence
without anger the farmin wasn't much anyway
and the school steady sayin vocational was secondrate to bein
four years gone and the dream of livin in a new
build blossomed blightwise after four year among similars

on an oxbow pretendin street named after an animal
you wouldn't know if it doctored yr eyes
in fact i think we've done it all
you and i alright tonight
tomorrow mornin someone always
bangin on chainlink
with ebay chainmail pajamas
percolator jammed with
flakin skidmark crayfish bygone six
season easy scum hyssop leaves
baby's binge rain
got a gutter butler salamander in it
whose bun bones are softer skin it
than the 6pack plastic rings
in the guts of the grizzly bear
gentile fingernail did you
one time play dead on the acid craw end
of a dirty bender ne'er-do-well??
and it all storms together childe
in the end's end's end yes it does
til then just keep
chewin on them reality tv keys
just til ruts run with bloodrain amen
lopin loosestrife got a burst name
and the eagles adamant as steel
angle down
unabashed unafraid winnin
my jig body bad tooth mornin
my every body step evidencing that

my goathead raw sashay to the farmers market
with the two canvas bags one larger
one smaller like a thought
and a feeling only
the other way around and a headache
from the night before
size of montana on meth
size of an empty mall
just this one store hangnail hangin on
what's to buy?? baby fart buttercorn scented candles
and xxlarge tshirts for 11month olds with inspirational slogans
misspelled markt down after the weddin
they three threw salt on ice
count of the slip steps down to the diced car
idling like a whale in a humane crockpot
baby on the way giveth a little kick
to the bassdrum bellybutton
in americay every 15 mins
one born screamin
may peg pierced asunder blues
one or the other parental hookt cheek
ass fat face to the opioid ahollowin
bonekin gutbound humanbein
supposed to be gravity prone
but drug got woodglue out
and stands wide a stance as a dish washer
riley see i seen a rooster die by rain and
i don't get paid nuff to risk boily privations
rain clear on thru the body

almost like get a glass jar fulla bacon grease
and ta take a dirty finger for a swim in it
see there's a limit to clean
in that sub sandwich line
gal pulls a birchlog of family orders
for every feral darryl here to bungo juice junkshun
and preens and cranes
just as finch in her glory three notes
for a babyhighchair who tells who
who is a stepstool?? keep her comin
to the mayo gun upside down in the parttimer'z paw
incest wrist tattoo couldbe scorpion
squeamish tadpole steamroll whale
mayo caulk caught a cold
a cloud hid a missile til
poundpound wetnose suffolk
turns out the price of noise and numb
is staggerin priest jackjim had him hymn laryngitis
and you could tell it cost a lot to sing
a brandy shake hand
hey he's doin his best autumn anythin
shakedown breakdown boated lip misses
hey snuff like dirt
spicy kind from quoted as holy graves
doubles his buttons likes he's buryin himself quarterways
evertime he reloads the lip
redrim eyes read 'em for dawn
or weary coal scuttle
based on how ya pooped this mornin

be well there in ditty
unrushed and sturdy as the sunflower
meant for somewhere and can i say it shinin
done nothin but react his whole measles tongue life
the old couch when you lift it
settling into its bones
foxy little weirdos everywhere you look
and we among 'em tear ourselves off a piece
of the problem flat rate flack flake
clack and wheeze
last bastard bread dough tooth
of toothpaste brought up to the tip
by the squeeze of a lifetime
is generous dope or it's more a feeling
like droppin railroad quartz and cinder in a skull hole
in skull holes don't help it see much
better dead plants fair to say
eau du dust
explode at the rate
of the spider war
garnishin the mall ice machine
get to it when they get to it
and when they do rumble
at the county park it's everybody now
stick the tongues of yr pockets out
don't need nothin but a car door
correct the saynay head ya either
come from here or ya don't
ya either pass the note or ya simmer over it

ya either catawba or ya hawkins
ya either coopt or ya prop
ya either dustercrop or featherduster
ya either antler for a windshieldwiper or stewball sapling
the meatballs were of tumbleweed and clay
if ya get my driftless popsicle
stick balsa wood flyer droppin
the sweat inside a dandelion knee
down thru yr dry eye spurn keen disposition
george washington in a rage throws
his aspen teeth
no oak teeth no teak teeth
no he didn't just say that??
o yes he id did there's
no more fearsome glue ma
than leopard eye sip at low slow shallow sleet
than cupboard chamber bole storm
than old sleetful snot ribbon rain
burning eyelid leopard loosestrife beeflake
every fire ever glance the wind
sets the teepee to sticks
here lies what once was a bobcat broom
and never shall there be much but jump mess again since
and soon sweet old cold chorus swings
into heated carpark view and
the seeing achieved then
goes the hill
elaboration drum dill
i open the flower and a flower

always i open the flower and a flower
whose tongues these are i think i know
three freepour doublez bein ideal
but then when i paint my life
the back of it the part i only dream i see
it's far too easy to shim off an eye
the very one that counts
and rub the paint bucket elbowwise
and stamp and jellyheadsmear
extra oblong grassfirecare mouths
come a hog nite when three siptowers
start the engine betides the juices
on the underside overpass overspill
henteeth memory hangnail globule
come on gone on all like a day
a getting thru morning really
hunchin past crystal shimmer
now there is the limo for hitchin
and there is the limo for deathspiritin
and the only difference is just
this slightest stationwagon feel
headburn wince lease
enhance it sunsun wachovia glass
corner of washington and 25th and migraine
downstream of the few jumpers of the 9am
market gun squeeze
jannnn heyy how are the veggies looking??
yesss see ya at the wedding reading farout friday ah
did you buy from my favorite mormons??

he seems to have an eye condition
least they are always irritated and
she seems to be the tree inside the tree
adieu adios eeyore bijou lightly
alone again heavy my eye
alone breath wheelbarrows lead filings peeperward
until i am eyenosing really
the pavement hoo holds up
bouquets of squeak and ganggold
i am not asking i am telling
to bowl the bowl of rented almonds
risks the party of
razorjaw dogs memorizing these epic grasses
i forget my first flower telephone
i forget being told i was born old i forget the moth
and mothball little too friendly
by god pee leg rabbit
don't care an ounce of once
for tightbound flounceful strayful crawl
by hopmeat yankyank
distance wean can't cain't
susan softest thought of dawn
fur lift by wind softer than the wind
and the wind yr mind makes packlock cyclone
when you finally make yr mind up
knew yaa had a new name comin
along or was grazing it
when yaa crockpotted his xxxmas robes
all day to cook the captious lazy out

what's left when sun pourz
last of the light and pines
take to dirting horizonlines??
why none other than one halfa
santabeard held to
anemia porchlite ma
linttrap hangin chads
bvd long mudsick path
why-me worm droolin from the lip
of this idiot starling
tinsel from the ass
of that vasekiller cat good nite
eye ream rest welsh knowin
we drag the diamond to gametime pure
with a rashy belly of chainlink that
drunk tool backt into after we booted him
for arguin bawls and shrikes and ifyuu
think there was 7up only in his handpinched can
then you must believe level-out lincolns
run on wildblursteam flintstone feet
or placed another way bananapeels
amplify the hayrick rot sink
choral spray gill scum cut of it
now did you just stick
that gumbo rue in yr uppers??
no but i did in the night
use for a snotrag these
underwear note the paralysis
along the inseam

stands for the flyover
in america
on diabetic halftoes
no sire only handout i ever
tookit was the tinnitus from the flyover
so no shithouse ever when dozed over
will tend to grow the sturdy flower
america your flowers do grow weak
in the doublejointed kneecaw
a craze of flies besets the punky
don't trust nothin into my maw
don't come with a lil teflon
starchin that checkered flag
fruit unpickt sits an old man
face on shoog belly bobolink behaves the sky
the butterfly besets the fleein fieldmouse
bird upon bank glass angst
breakneck ball palmed
of ransomed beauty
let this poem pal w/ gentlefoot god
reader deer don't the rain get in
yeer bubblegum machine mind times
more need spleen yellow
gobsmack black never
meant to be seen static daisyface neon
still finch hey slow this hair part down
prone knife crayoned with margarine
death renders everyone open object for eye pry
and here comes the poem upon

slippery glitz where you stand
comes from givin those pompons
the royal treatment
with a late springtime attitude
bird bank to you
windows must have seemed endless cerulean
a perfecter bribe none can what
bit what blind what off argentine
phosphene falling
guy golden cy twombly stolen
press this watch dead why
to the chest because
halfway down
the singer's throat
and backing out
yellowjacket i call out bee to
done we are destined to
sweeten
sweets to the living a while
swept again
set against some little helpers even
select for inside you there is no inside
you why not let honey ride ma
floods the carpet impossible heavy
my sore low back kind lay out
receipts for coasters
ah but for what you owe and pay
ape paper's too thin to outpace the damps
the damned good times too many to count

after great tombs of blues
to see ya haa again i don't even
hear it while it's happening avalanche
of ants all my own
internal gleebomb shake it down
to first music of a day to
the little salted cowbell chickadee call
to chickadee call to chickadee
in spume of sawdust
cartoon swedish lumberjack
holds out a finger and the jolly bird
broughts its twitch there
lighter designed to burn the birch too quick there
bird broach lightswitch there
vole teeth corked from possum teeth pliered from
skunk crazy for chickens
wrapped in plastic owl foil
aw cross the span of boo
earth in our time
beyond time nuclear yoyo
heated so freezin takes skin
with every idle slap of the ham
of the hand old blood keats
keeps reachin 65 percent mestic farm farters
32 percent human fuckers 3 percent
or less everyone else insects crashin oceans
crashin birds long about a third
in the gut of never come again
how are we then so

blood loud smug log?? cup up
a fart from below and whiff it
for news or good or bad?? it's all
in the smell gut's lonely road
framed by numb arm arch ditches is it
armistice if the bombs are just
sleeping?? dirt itchy fitful sapling jacked
on pulpmulch of heartattacked humminbirds
see what you got is a skunk problem
gettin in among the chickens
i can see it on yr niteshade hat from miles away
in among the gourdish garden
in a starin contest
with a toad if you ever have watched
a fair thee well warted one proceed
then you've seen how a wallet will
topple nudgled forward towards
the lights of dallas one
2 3 2 bitter rootz casting
at a time shoots of sweet in quotes so green
there's somethin
about a twang gets yr heart
up on the fulcrum of the knee
and presses down
ecstatic agony comes to mind
trenchant grapefruit head squeezed
by russian outofwork guitarhero
took the hack work cuz she could
get it

pull yr own teeth with
a needlenose
trump tomorrow gonna
blow some fracksand up
yr asshole keepin us out of
foreign wars and savin babies cryin
like babies lockt in school closets
the gun beyond closer
goin blam faster how can it faster
than yr heart goin so fast the beats melt into one
sustained udddd he's handin out
upside down big mack leviticuss
to them clemson tackle boys main thing is
give 'em what they are used to
roadconcrete more
than any swirlin keyhole wind
there's a watertank says never minds it
smell bothers ya just hold yr spiritus
and kwaff that border dew wrench
could be years you just get used to it
steppin around where it's wet
blood'll go to yr head
you get to playin bird
stoopless at the tank
pinball in there to season the zero stew
the crockpotted morningglory
the coonskincap phone glass toilet
formered in the rind frame
wing always so personal

bad check you ooph feel
in the longer foot bones
churches lichens
soldier crawl cross
new wise eyewasht arise and see
dragonfly from cattail
lightswitch from lacquer
cur from cursory
leer from lurch burr
once live lunch god is
from whose soft stalk parted i pay my
contemporary sturdy way
the audience stirs
in their seats it's
their undies caught up a little
on fold and curve of future grub
yes this curtain is
cake if yr willin to
throw yerself thru
worship warship unsink the give
us up each other by the billion galleons
us trackin a cousinly friend on that phone app and
when it comes to you dancin on the median mitchell
believe you me behold the skyway for the dotdot
will be becoming this parttime farmer
runt with a lotta bad knees this
sunflower parachute is a one drop deal only getting tired
of playin 7th fiddle to pirate's froze eel cane
see here he's at walmart

cart fulla wine sounds like
waterglass cupboard in the prelude
to the big one earthquake quake
buyin frozen dinner punched
33 not 3 minutes and the thing
exploded polly pocket cricket pieces everwhere
had to take a butterknife to to try and
pry off because he whipped
to mcdonald's right after that boom
everything dried to honest stone boom
and he hammered a hole accidental boom
with the knife them cypress gnarl powerful hands
and did i knowthink it was safe to run
a wave even just a little with a hole in its inside??
best leave this one here here
honey i hold i hope you find it
when you mosts need it
i hole you walk it to the barndoor
off its hinges whose crooked laughter
is made by the wind that made it limited
i hope you throw it know it high i home the bats react
when shovel the snow no that's that cottonwood cat dander
doin the kerosene tongue tinder trampoline 'pon your heart
and lifting into right
angles your arms
pump them
rise as you fall
forgive everyone
yourself in there on the outside

of the circle piss they w/ rust
suds in the snow jerk no that's
rows of pissin lightnin bugs with their fuses
rubbed off along the gums no the cheeks
of them wild boloney roughhouse stooges
some obnoxious insult only you would get
gets those smoky spindle ears of yours little fires to smokin
rip a rib them
kidney drawl acid words pokin
at yr gutsick with a goddamn icicle
no a buffalo gut finger fine
got hard smash cat rise syrup rise
look yonder down the skinny barrel
of years pants pulled down
on bull shame's a fence
on fire don't you wish
was once that wide for purposes of
tractor and haybine brother i hate
to tell this you but every human
if you get to lookin long at the particulars
sodbound bud pull off where at??
in tha cornfield stubble
nothin but sapsucker noshave saplings
getting their ghostcroquet hogwallow snipfit goin
where there is no gate this is go time
there found ta be beatin softenin head
meth gainst meth no meth square meth
deal glue wheel i can't uncuck
loosenin t00th on each

piece rides a flea jit jitney
that the backhoe cuts holes??
course i am say-s the metal
tho i'd prefer be a professional
chocolate drop
lickin her chops
codgers they did use to be
just shy of numberless dead jan to may
in wisco of opiated humheart stone
and earth say-s half into a theatre
pete seeger cronkite bone
yes i can see it with none but my knuckbone
you hath smucker eyes i
or fire shall get high on
eat of swoon aging bein bring the stethoscope
more and more up to clock
the tree in the tick tree
and the paintin under the paintin
can just feel there's a gummy fence down in
that man's apple render
o won't we almost make an us
spend an okay time
meaty meteor snores froggy skip it hearts
toady ticket toes
my god my skin sky for a time
size of the yard
sleeping in the sighin yard tree
o god so hungover tomorrow
jaw hurts burps hurt bad banana skins

old ones tied around my neck tied
around my waist paranoid astronauts
at happenstance hotel tonight
was it spread eagle on tarmac was you
pullin a willie nelson?? while mail planes
docile as algae luncheon carp
our sweepstakes inside
turn fane and what??
get the wax out
turn fin and wane
meankindtime nineteenthhole neaptide
creeps up on the dipper's lip
and the plainsmen news reports
in between the no times to
come times for the fayuckt farm times says
we are the new faces of the watertowers
how you like that uu and ii
ps maybe aint gotta use a clotheshanger
and a cruelness for flyswatter going forward
us outside the usa in it just by lookin up
unreasonably happy on this polyurethane porch
grand island ne come a night middle march
the cranes carry only themselves and another
hobo song how pure to lonely no more
how perfect like no other
how rite wright right their
songs bein ragged hugged
out of 'em drunk squeezes compliments
of dave marr streetlight moonlight athens georgia

it's truer trees nearer streetlights keep
their leaves on longer just sayin
and they later are too
the liar will
wear hiz R2D2 way
straight through the wuther true
and no there ain't nothin ancienter than
the bedbug termite wallboard nightlight and
yes it is possible to see the moon for the first time too nigh
them cranes'll make you redream like that
are the scissors to the fingers of the sailors
moon about a baby did you port of
hangup on my lately origami jailer??
gum disease cheat sheet landlord
dogfoods splint the hearts of whalers
bad baby cookie was the captain's heeler
or cookie for short or cuckold for shortening
if the so-called bindin agent is fake it
til you make it ma then crumble cuz
the cusser and the kisser called off
the wagon had the haul real tin roof feel in real time go
what it woulda made us?? the wittol haul
the bootleg stuff chucklin all cluckcluck in the barrel
it's best not to think on
there's a price for even thinkin
awhile more and you'll sleep
in the aisle at the buck a dvd
outlet vape life see that's
just steam comin outta there sayeth

the frogleg with 7 eye on and it's over for true
doll when ungrammatical feels darin
when the gal text factory and the guy
poison shingle stew comin up from
under old mill river gorge bridge local
they say ya hear a baby swear
paintcan astronaut ocelot helmet
hellbent on a telegraph stop
entire woods lost stop
we heard it before we come up upon it stop
where once this pewtree there stood
a musical saw in places any more
and they was all tuned to nirvana stop and there wasn't
nothing at all to stop it stop cry into stop
so folks went ahead stop and boohooed
into the peetie wheatstraw static shock hair of the child stop
one bus seat in front stop slight slight case of urine
and the light turns yellow green
and the child got that detention blackboard eraser
chalk all over her spy glass
has ha been saving
old snow in a glove and the glove
havin untold power wet child says dryly
who died and made you the unofficial
emperor of mourning?? unbends turnin
and slappin slaps yr nose right off
yr snoot there paper cranin to the green cream plastic floor
to the loose fallen hairs and powdered fritos in shapes
of musical notations come again and heel

there's a pencil going clear through the green vinyl
a couple seats ahead rat kid pulsates it in in and
out and in when anybody gets home to crockpot something
lewd at the last
just if a sliver a livin salamander
just if the offender don't got a fox cun cuttin blisters
on the tar side of the moon at his groinspout
then i didn't just write this allll as a air-
hug lavisht upon that fuckin foolllll
feel me foe?? nothin just?? nyet gist rye
trouble no more trouble with me
i ain't got no governero
see it comin no stoppin
only part of that man ever a brake
heart only one i knew
to choose the straight and narrow life
was the funeral train well
well possum quick swigs tuesday
rain from ditched beandip can
gets eaten hotdog contest style by again
the chorus world record dreamed
whole dang song is you just keep on
with the same hawtdawg phrase
rat up smyrna way
in jeans with the holes factoried in
designed it thataway
great lost chin off god store is
tooth pain layin on a dodge ram horn inside
guy behind the counter could be tibet

or malaria methy bigots even do their former church
pleases here is savins of seven cents
on the dollar so why do all the bathrooms
in truckstops in tennessee feel
like the ideal of an angel got lost
in the undercover hover of this racquet ball
racket for wings fly?? hospital
eventual heard that jigsaw bird
singin key clean tile and it's the hour between
rooster and chicken and wolf and dog and
the cello is a river and the river is yr hair
and the handsize waterbed boxwine hung
people's radio willow dollar hopes
up upon redder redder ears
underwater underwear white whiter
nervouser hands made for gathering
what was there last time
i herd more the gaps
in grasping than anything sure
bunched blur carry water in bag
wild at heart apple
rain lashin down sideways for straight on
maymay make a fat lip
of myshirt and sack out to carry home
ah but them apples they got that inborn squirm
keeps you on yr toes
things tipping lock topple lark start daze
in my knees oceans in the fields feel
how impossible the windrow

'thout grunt and reach
of machine ma and what we can hold
if only for short times surprises
way handwashed shirt does
wring these pulses these these
held in what holds us fall
with an all at onceness
you ill you weller meld mirror
smokeless tobacco minor key tile sit up love life
make a short speech the weather
run a green yarn through father
old flighty got a fallback callback and they order
be at the backdoor at a quarter to
but watch them alleycats healed natural
by wind and time little wet rub
on chainlink chops it all down ever get to
thinking of everything one time??
made by mophead and mopstick touchin
mossy moped needs a new rear wheel
aren't you now speakin for every
blur eye farmer weighs the options
makes fast the rope?? this here mow
used to be hay by the mile
a field a baked bread
crosseye cats crisscrossin them bales
in a heaven of instinct i dream a tom
with 19 legs i dream he goes sideways in reverse
lake ice that grand ass portmanteau y'all
i dream an great horn owl oven built

stone bread we tear into when that taste
no longer spalls the stoke hole by first light
will be seen we have haloed our plates
with the littlest bones there was that old??
was it yesterday?? was it late last night??
saturday night live joke?? about i
crush your heads?? and we remember that
nickingly taking these mice-n regrets just out back
after all it's ass biting out breath glaucous shawl
going up there's a lungbreathbathrobe 7 feet above
there's nothin at all pinch each one breaks
and crumbles sufficient to enter 'braska snow
as snow whose crackle and squeak
is all one going to be alright
runs good decent tires great brakes
as for the famous flood this car dodged that
was on a crazy ass errand for my schemin
dad somethin about a goat with
perfecter sheep dna
only thirsty ribs keep heat
cold keeps stone and that's the end
or close to this sermonia i told you once
i told you an hundred times i been
readin with mirrors
been in comely wicker
hives for centuries survived his life tho
dad did his homemade tattoos harder to say
one's a line bending toward nowhere
either that's pure limpid possibility

or dead grass beat duncely by this dog
going along express to pass mean on
comes apart when hungry just like you
playin backgammon against the snow
dandelion fluffs on the underside of ol snoozy
morsel eye fawn love comes
sudden unexpected let
love love you harder if
yr heart's an extended if if if stay motel
whose pun for stoppin off along the way
has what?? pus in its plant leg
someone coughin?? or was that laughin??
fernet tongue hard as a gas pedal
turned blue by tv's excoriating 'plause
and you can hear it ma with yr trick ear even
the miscreant dewdadism aw shucks'in
in the splay teeth rake for whom one
long look could amount to pullin johnny
cash out of american flag compression sock branson mo
blends with the little cusses of the man fennelin yr prayer
towns and thrift store prom gowns away
got gas on his good jeans overflowed the leafblower
knows it without thinkin it will be days
before light flames' lazy magnet
slopt top lighters matches
won't lean a little in
small town turned herd heads
static electric cats tick along walls
'course the willow writing iron grate fancies

meow meow sea dice merle
in slate of foam fuss river had to ask had to ask why he
why was he withy wearin those at all??
rain rain filament filibuster the pane pain
bark barks saddle the dusk the rusky rusk dusk
alarum be your pledging gait
and my hard as talc
in a thunderstorm dream devolves
now first thing the dawn does is rub
some robbed of their water
tomatoes along the cheekline
next up is cauterize cobalt
hard to get this kind to mean
much into play clay balls lust got shaped
clays placed at serious intervals shut that gate
on the dark woods hay mow floor hey hey
let shook out chaff dust be the eyes
and placed there deft as fieldstone
on a fool post next thing the dawn does is
soak the ricepaper in salmon juices
oil fidgets under ground
adam extracts it yes he will
greed's a bag husked yes it is
and the sound of dead birds can i get an open d
for the turning in the bag now
don't you worry
this disgusted dog
met you before bite he don't
got a tartar sauce justice mask for a nose

went on and learned
rub an oak to bone to warm
god indulge the woodpecker
doltish by head wham and in
need of cool counterpoise
who is going to save you now
badass blackeyed susan??
begs to differ diffidence can fuck off her neither
of the ditch nor sideroad nor field pose
course far be it for a seed to yessir rightofway bylaw
put it this way pard mayberry daymay
no county truck cames
no brute sets a poison's crawl
ta scythe it all down this i know
the red look it
numbers telling me
it's early still and there is time still
for massacre and children
whose glass cheeks let you see
the laugh coming up
ahead of time growing up
there was nothing like the mail
there could be anything often nada
before love drama mail scratched my
yearn scat into a cathedraled hill
i took to climbin soon as i could stroll
funny how we sneak up on things
wouldn't mind it
often a spider livered in the back

and creeper yarn eggd it up
ants and sodas of 'em
spuming along the jaw
squeaked whined winced
between bored boy bats
and everyday pulling on
i guess you'd say endangered
crockpot pry to prion metal ma
took to the sonic shape of its use weary
sloop weary sloop and i have no doubts
the insides got to be kolache knee completely
satisfied with the dark
the floodin river by the leading
backup singer in case
you didn't hear it had the voice
settlin like ghee along the bone
most tantamount
to breeding success these days
i am not opposed to makin clothes
from those smoke break curtains
that stain there is
on account of overample elbow sweat
a whoosh sir pry floursack
flags of it stuttering
down inverse moat
bloat no piranhas nor
mercenary mercury perches
raisin their flowerfastbacks
in the gutted ridges todayyy

once young seven paces
from the box 7 year old i shot a catbird
on a powerline with a bbbbb
flounced off the belly of that
ditch water bird came arching back
to rest in my left earrrr
random punctuation
you must've fallen asleep
your hands pressing the keys
vigorouser in the deepgone
like this 230948023984oweirafsdfj
at the time i had a handsome ache from river
water in the other you can't make
this shit up this morning one catbird feather
sleeps light in the dijon arms of susan's wide smile
bow out across the sun
scratches out a melody
all you want you'll have harmony
air somewhere right here
the tires are burning
with the patience of parents
of potatoes growing so
very very slowly around
armchairs stones
tones in toebones waitin
for them dewclaw matchsticks
ride the holy shake smokes
evel knievel in a licked onesie
opens up his arms

honey i appreciate u surrender
when all the ant sun loinz razzle in
no mail for least another hour say
no turkey dust tails yonderer
who knows nose blows cries the memory
of the maniac at the handpumpwell
city park done away with them years ago
guess the assgrab mayor got constipated on seein people
wet question what's the sound of the wind
across a parkin lot?? answer human
misprision pissant stew of barking sticks and
since when does mutton breath click??
go and try and rest yr ant pants head on a declawed bible
whose damper bursting farts
hearten the spines of impolitic roses
airy mayhemy with doily
bad check signed with meth heart
man shot dead
by a mini series of clothes pins
we play the slow arrow out the heart
useless beat up like that
guess you could step on it
and outsource tha gutbucket sound
with the live feed coughin on grain dust behind
just like us to do that save the date
for first last gasps our sweetly
reckless need to say we were in on it
is well recorded on the face lines
of frowning mothers used to

our ostentation potentation
start the fire all over just by
looking of course yes our eyes are
magnifyin glasses and the hour is highish noon
and it's in its torture nature to get away
fire feral up the 1legs
of the mailboxes here to the turnin in the road
wraps itself around anaconda
in a youtube until the toasted chars
suck sand of ash down
the sears a deal open new again penneys too
downtown upstands ben franklin
straight from the box twinklin new
and the kids skinny up walk
backwardz from kkk burb glands
their depends undergar suddenly frozen milk
it's good to feel familysize again hands now
what just sang?? the wind sang
cracked up by ha hat peaks
and what is this dust??
why crickets ma
dismantled by season
grounded to life different
and when we dream??
yes fresh cricket sand crawls in
to correct our teeth
plumps our gums
polished to blind nickel
given us for free fine dream kid

but we'd stilla been poor
as chaucer's bones
stranger than seashells
in mountain clefts
wedged in
whose spirals cement
the water down the drain mirage
whose puckered burl
translates this way
belly button tie off
time's a fucker after
i grow old not knowing
yes feather yanked
from the still warm
raptor wing passed
over and over the body
what is it keeps you up
at night?? literal sighs
maybe coordinated
snowflakes
stark dorks
of wind nudgin us
to the center
of the sidewalk
and down spiral lost tool road
talkin gossip soppin
with saw teeth
sneaky soft in blue lube
or do y'all walk right

through your regrets??
i see it like this pete says while we
settle in the mud
and the sky back stays freaky hairy
on geese hustle future scuppernong
hour spines stretching
to the yahonkin brawlings
we are all atoms on loan
and i don't know about you
but i am lookin forward
to gettin back into circulation
see he come up upon and to the house
and drew water up
out of me dot sez he he liket it
every harvest times after
ever to mess around on me
and what i heard was
dot 4square swears it
his heart stop ping
from up atop me
frazy cast as
a hummingbird
i am unafraid to tell it
up a bobcat's ass
and then negligible
a dog lickin itself
only grows the thirstier
and then was gone
yes it was like sometimes

strike the like them spring snows
or how the creaking
new marriage bed
of the old windmill
is also a closed
house of stone
and some mornings
yes i am not afraid to tell it coming as he was going
had to pry him off
like i've heard the people do
the oysters off the rocks
and when i'd lain him aside
thick and bony same mattery time
rocky rock rockin chair
on its side
needs some working on
i knew it was no point in screaming
the luck clock steady goin
someone walking
last snow of the season
guess i never knew
time's plod til then
and i only younger since
that trapper looks too good too
to me
seems ribs see
are plenty fierce fencing
for one honest american
carolina's famed night fauna

cougar moon i hum that song
the oo-wa of it all
the metal clasp shinin
had a dream the trapper gem
gave birth to overhauls i swear it
and a feather out the cougar ass
is just natural way he'll fly a little
etc yr lustrous texas inseam etc
old bending of the roads
perfect pitch some folks bend forks
for magic me i mend
black out dream roads
birch bark piano for free
and what did we hear early??
roadway singin from that shit bag hotel
right like hotter water you say
in a doublerboiler doin the grits deed
whale angina i say and fan the heat
rash slap shaping up weedily
exactly nevada under my left
nipple seasons
and snowmelts then
from roofs snug with snow
mountains ancient with it
a road a vinyl groove i sing it
like a crowwing shingle ya use to fan yrself
at the funeral for attention
moving itch inch plays us something
simpler coyer than dead and

sometimes it seems
the stars we worship
simper down and bathe
in the rot of
a fresh fresh dead death thing
and rise
not quite themselves
ain't that like tv luv
shell out
the beak break
hustle shrunk eyes
my favorite hunt
gone eye larking
among parlor oriented trees
gone skeletal
whose last leaf
might still be on
evanescent childe
as stalwart evansville exit
granulated thru fever sheets of rain
call that what you like all i know
is river welcomes it this heron too
cured from her meanstreak
by blowin basil smoke up her nose
on down the tightrope of
hwy 61 safest neighborhood around
even the strays fat as tumor rumors
carried by saints
in plastic shoppin bags

no them they satcheled in sheep afterbirth
run thru a bleachin trough special designed
to let young inside ghost out
you had ghost old
newspaper turned ambrosia
in the gutters of yr purple house
i knew it then people talk about keyed up
how you are house driven nail mishit shit
crooked lock on every room ah but
you are all the keys asleep on a deadhead nail
or is most everything in life is it begrudging??
and why won't you come out the bathroom??
city lights insomniacing the sparrow shadow
your succulents hold up your weedsmoke
a little more loose those bags are prunes of
sewer water under the sparrow's eyes
it should be we smell of thick stale smoke everywhere
it should be people know us with their nose as
survivors of stars reached their iron dippers
down our drawers and paladiums of frictions later
here we are in the clearing buzzin and saturnine
to the touch butcherin cacti for the starvin cattle
it's not hunger it's thirst it's not thirst it's
a letter in the shape of a curse they were all there
all good there bent over plenty wedding the stone serrated
exercises a bind the cut cared for pulls apart
like fiction it's true tho
bent over out of balance
almost out of breath against you

pulled across a parked el dorado i cured
the urge to burp by there's black earth
down in the moon you just gotta dig down
backwards cacaw your coo moan trill
i hear it still in the absence
on the wren branches in the receipt lint that flies
from my poutin pockets like
shit in a bag from a window in edinburgh in
1339 from this thrift store harmonica
lucky harp flooded grand coulee dam
curry crystal lunch breath lucky
squeezed offwhite horizon
horicon spurts the egret
as in wickset morel stay
in range and unafraid and
january crapz a pistachio dish ma
of cedar waxwings spiraling sideways again
yes net they down again
see no rope floats long without something
buoyant in between
ah the waxwings in between today
card the berries today
wool to way today
walk warmly today
and freely today
cart cartwheel today
son house today
wants be baptist
preacher so i don't

have to work
bar to church to bar
blood in barks embarking
upon what do you see??
upon my neck of blood
steady and pained and freeing
always saucy always
rockin seashell eye
baby don't never let
your sands cop
pitch petrify
these berries easily
1/7th the size
of this birded body
held an instant
as tho the all of bird
gets to weighing the wax
left unhissed in candle
birded body
rubber as seal
if i might pinch you
you might squeal
static unioning
the state of the balloon
these birds these berries
girding gearing
and with scrolls for skits
fotobombed by fleas'
fitful ass spastic

this one foxy one
raccoon cough of wing
so close to my skin
her hand there down at its tip
it is purpling i can't get that
out of my head dipped in wine purple
all blood relinquishing hold
worse things than dying
gramsy your heart
to go home to
how last steps rests steeps
when you enter as in
bingo parlor lite there's
the holy water dip
down to the first knuckle
and absent swipe
the forehead
i feel it the wind now
who would like bereavement snacks??
from boozy berry wrung
tornado vestment
warray alley allay
and cooled and heheated
toe a heel away we
going cooing cooling this
many one more
two gingko leaves
fallen in tandem
so as to seem two

thoughtful thoughts
in butter sweaters
i love you
ruined to sepia
solestruck
flount the shuns
cummerbund the halfwind
the cairn sure to croon
so why not livbig?? my personalized
license plate get this is messssss
what we did was walk breezy into
the party wane and just jumpstart it act naturally
fella with a future cut over his left eye and barbedwire
spiderweb tatts on his armpits you could see
when the lonely beauty song come on
shuts his eyes and swhirls
a lasso of the mind tossin it
in the end over end half them phonecheckin
chairsitters play the laws baby
of wide nets and sun bloodlets
the wind carries down on stretchers
the river wretches down to green
the creek runs but once per year gangrenous splurges
vintage to nobody out this county road
livin as we do in an honor or else clamp county
what side are you on?? sez the cave
is deeper than sound and you'd hate to die
bailing the waters of regret from the walmart
totes unbelievably can go green

is slime is getting and putting too fine a point on it
yes in the not so distants when
walmart and amazon get their
merger britches on and every sec
you even think about what you might
want it drops on your house head from
drones quiet as the last of something
that's how my felonious cousin
makes a killin see
whim bomb roofs
this pinch it it's real toothpick
here is attributable burble to the actual jesus
baby manger wood just think about it
shooing stuck meat with a lord kid whale
killer in miniature do they now??
do the rabbits in the rabbit
in the dog's dream feel
the sand train devil may carin?? and
is it in the baby rabbit's first hoppin??
frack song train oblivion
boom it til ya bust it boom til ya bustard
neither fancy tipsy kite nor licorice yoke
yorick pobre tasteless eyelash fruitfly for halo
in corking flight all life gift got a temp
job in a v and goin down
battery shit it
isn't it rage and joy live
as one in the same yotel pigknuckle about
3 and 3/4 ways up the spine?? no tellin

petrol gargoyle when the great oink comes
come on be off
this house meaning
my body needing
a wrinkled font to
john the prine end
i do i bake a bread
of how you run
no up to huff
real afraid wild sparrow birds
their midas leaping
rats from cindered ships
soothed some
the ghosts give
the soft rock
of yr pocket cloth
perfectionisms
let you alone let anyone
to the soft of my tongue
the locked rocks of me
the names rubbed free
by storms and by suns
country quiet all
lichen knee bear
about to bream back
out of the drug
of rain moil leaf breath
it is said to be
soporific the wound

raw and creaking
they then laid the damp
leaves against
and i was sealed
something in the blu shed
shouting good god
it was a mummer play imagined
by the snake in the aquarium
i swear to it ate the rocks
it was an inside the parker in the making
the ball bounding laughingly
under his glove
whereas men were useless
oaken poultice
pondered the whisperings
of the reeds and set the spike song
all donkey humble hauler protectorate
okay again awhile
flock seed wonk so soon
farm kids make duck heads
of their calf snot hands
and calling to the others
those shoring shiverers
for whom entry
is always entry is always toe to
meniscus torture me
slay slow alarm my
ah into the corrugated shine
on two some rocksolids dive

their heels russet golds
their heels alonely ma
breaching the darker
inks of water
and mustard glass
of light upon
the swelling water
then turtles in unison
blown to the surface
disperse handless clocks
passage rocked
is is is
i answer the phone
like this because
my underwear
are those abandoned
overburdened winter
babybucket parkswings
swans mostly
caught between a cartoon
and the real thing
bedaggered with
red red autumn
until the wind yes until the wind
unsure of the year anymore
it is almost spring's first fallwintersummer silly
and we all hunkered like limpid prawns
inn quiet upkey anti physicality rooms
sworked up own chests brinks

in edgy vigil ville
furnitured by
shallow breaths
adjusting our own
into the in between
in the commercial forever
calgon take me upbraid
butter park K sadness tho
at times a wind inflating
leaf into dogeared ecstasy
just as stillness strangely
propels the rain
woman winner you
in a man's boots whose
winter red hot tapwater hands
spirit chick like flame
and can rattle whistle
spot-on guinea mimic
let alone none approach
the baronheart trees
out glass sand shook stirrin wheels
out wheels and boils out reeds pvc boys
dirty flower forth
none lovely weird grr louder than
the watchdog guinea hen
herself a flame turnin in
the purple suck cheek
of her splendor while
slop and grain strews

how to say bird expands
in birdly revolution
satin cape bull
inside the bull
the bull of wind
daughter stutters thru
workshirts by the collars
under deeper than is easy
to care for without dreamy thinking water
outside of town purple marten
plastic pistol mumped with prune
iron this this darl a way the clay's
himped drawls i mean
resist the flat grunts rest here
if only sweet summertime
if only wholesome if only atmospheric
only soulful and in need of gravy
o kick up a cheese dross shad
tent's thins snored exposure
dissemblin fleetfoot ten
mazy may daisy tin
bent ample by the pilly wind
so no lawn so song swan saw
so bare bide so blue
this flame fright jazz hand gesture
is so for calmer-ing you
you and yeer warm flour hairs
bob as you dash rubberband tan
stretched to snap before the the the

face primp shrink shrike drinker father
bob as u dash a dash shook the plain vine sugar
only gramsy knew what pinch that is
tarragon a swell soundin libel
and she now a flower
unspeakably yellow
always i draw the flower
its sack a lake dance
banana dipped in yokes
from chicken wire aprons robbed
by wind's heady enticements
dashes like a dashed
javelin upon the battlefield
of the sentence as it is wise suspension
she said are you going to church
she didn't ask slow as the cat
is dead and the earth
lushes her comforting name
clay slow furniture
how i came to breathe
crane canary stovepipe
breath link brain chain
when proffering this circle
take it in hand in hand and
tear raggedly free
unsteady stirring
gets a stick
in the river
a kid a clock a face

odd how tug can be
a settling rounder this
is your comfort soup
take and eat
she says and i do and i
never had anything
other than the only thing
i almost had
says the incorrigible gravel to the criminal wind
greens or reds it's yours to choose
only neither'll turn over in this cold
barns rutabagas rhubarbs
rise as they fall
dig tow unfurl
coal floral train curling
the frack you mean ma
the middle is ours
sweet meat heat heat here here
tomorrow is early
tonight's high noon
our legs don't have to be
tables swallowed by elbows
the windows jerking with strangers
we can go can go there
opposite direction
the winded window teaches ends
can go there by feel and
be known for love
gonna turn it all around

once i kill this gate
this the lifted river
crawling this the stick
this the waxwing's triangle head
leaned against another
that's the square
deal song of the wine
her dead hand made
grounded muse most musical
oven mitts for mittens
backlit by sun
eaten by oceans of cold
she then angels upon
the setting one
jelly thin best spread it thick
and i begin
again to sing
into the burdock's 100th velcro eye
weirdo deer to you
for you

Acknowledgments:

Very special thanks to BJ Hollars at Hope Is The Thing (WI Historical Society Press, 2021); to Christopher Chambers at Midwest Review (2021); to Ashley M. Jones and Rebecca Gayle Howell at What Things Cost: an anthology for the people (University of Kentucky Press, 2022); and to Chet Weise at Third Man Books (2021) and the Literarium at Third Man Records London, where the very start, the very end, and some of the slaloming mayhem in between, first found hostals.

Through whom in whom:

Monica Detra, William Detra, Linda Detra, R Smith, Erin Kavanagh, Meggan & Eddy Meisegeier, Angus & Rosy & Pippin Meisegeier, Joy Detra, Jane & Bob Detra Davenport, Pam Carazo, Larry Matuszewski, Steve Timm, Shari Bernstein, Scott McWaters, Deb Davidovits, Matt Harle, Eric & Ivet Parker, Mark & Jim & Eva Schultz, David Floyd, Warner Moore, Ashley Durant, Joel Brouwer, Michael & Marilee Wutz, Tom & Kyra Hudson, Greg Brownderville, Erica Revak, Chet Weise, Linda Harrison, Tim Earley, Emily Wittman, Craig Pickering, Jason Busse, Courtney Craggett, Heidi Lynn Staples, Ander Monson, Don Revell, Sandra Simonds, John Pursley III, Adrian Kien, Shelly Taylor, Matt Patton, Scott Hunter, Bill Pfalzgraf, JM Wilkinson, Ashley Chambers, Susi Wiesner, Bronson Tew, and Jerry Goldberg.

Especially:

Gratitudes immeasurable to the shining folks at Propeller: Dan, Jan, and Lucas.

Abraham Smith is the author of numerous poetry collections—most recently, the chapbook *Bear Lite Inn* (New Michigan Press, 2020), the full-length *Destruction of Man* (Third Man Books, 2018), and *Dear Weirdo* (Propeller Books, 2022). Away from his scampers and desks, he improvises poems inside songs with the Snarlin' Yarns; their debut record *Break Your Heart* was released on Dial Back Sound in Fall 2020: thesnarlinyarnsut.bandcamp.com. He lives in Ogden, Utah, where he is associate professor of English and co-director of Creative Writing at Weber State.

IN THE PROPELLER BOOKS CONTEMPORARY POETRY SERIES

Kirsten Ihns, *sundaey*

Abraham Smith, *Dear Weirdo*

www.ingramcontent.com/pod-product-compliance
Lightning Source LLC
Chambersburg PA
CBHW032046290426
44110CB00012B/979

9 780982 770481